# The Mighty Pterodactyl

Percy Leed

LERNER PUBLICATIONS ◆ MINNEAPOLIS

**Note to Educators**

Throughout this book, you'll find critical-thinking questions. These can be used to engage young readers in thinking critically about the topic and in using the text and photos to do so.

Lerner Publications Company
An imprint of Lerner Publishing Group, Inc.
241 First Avenue North
Minneapolis, MN 55401 USA

For reading levels and more information, look up this title at www.lernerbooks.com.

Main body text set in Helvetica Textbook Com Roman.
Typeface provided by Linotype AG.

**Library of Congress Cataloging-in-Publication Data**

Names: Leed, Percy, 1968– author.
Title: The mighty pterodactyl / Percy Leed.
Description: Minneapolis : Lerner Publications, [2022] | Series: Bumba books - mighty dinosaurs | Includes bibliographical references and index. | Audience: Ages 4–7 | Audience: Grades K–1 | Summary: "Pterodactyl wasn't a dinosaur, but it lived when dinosaurs did. From its four legs to its long beak, this fascinating flying lizard is sure to capture any dino lover's attention!"— Provided by publisher.
Identifiers: LCCN 2021010496 (print) | LCCN 2021010497 (ebook) | ISBN 9781728441061 (library binding) | ISBN 9781728444475 (ebook)
Subjects: LCSH: Pterodactyls—Juvenile literature.
Classification: LCC QE862.P7 L44 2022  (print) | LCC QE862.P7 (ebook) | DDC 567.918—dc23

LC record available at https://lccn.loc.gov/2021010496
LC ebook record available at https://lccn.loc.gov/2021010497

Manufactured in the United States of America
2-1008741-49721-8/11/2022

# Table of Contents

# Flying Reptiles

Pterodactyl was a flying reptile.

It is extinct.

It was not a dinosaur.

But it lived when dinosaurs did.

Can you name any dinosaurs?

Pterodactyl was the size of a chicken. People have found fossils of flying reptiles. Fossils show an animal's size.

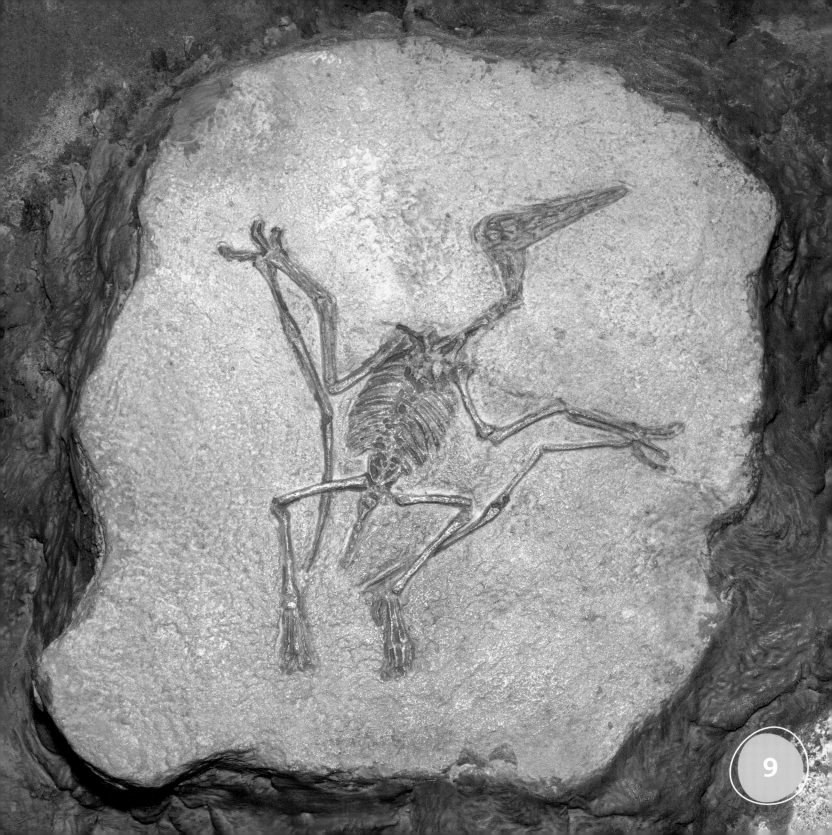

Flying reptiles had wings.

They were made of skin.

Flying reptiles had beaks.

Beaks helped them catch fish.

Many flying reptiles

had head crests.

These could be big

or little.

crest

15

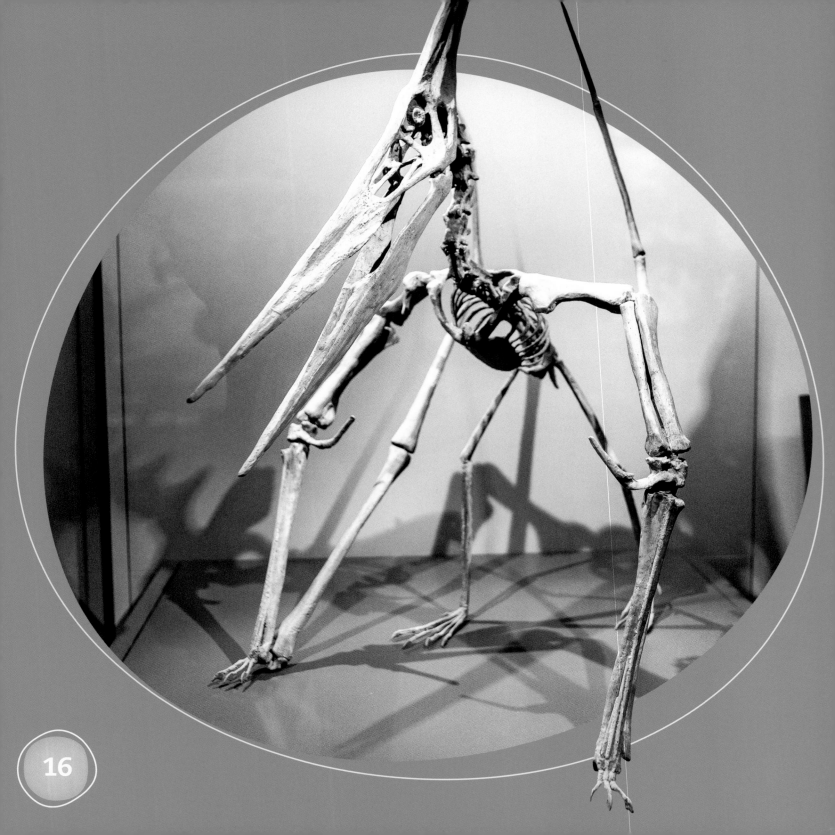

Sometimes flying reptiles walked.

They walked on four legs.

They made nests.

They laid eggs there.

Most flying reptiles

lived in groups.

How many flying
reptiles do you
see in this group?

# Parts of a Pterodactyl

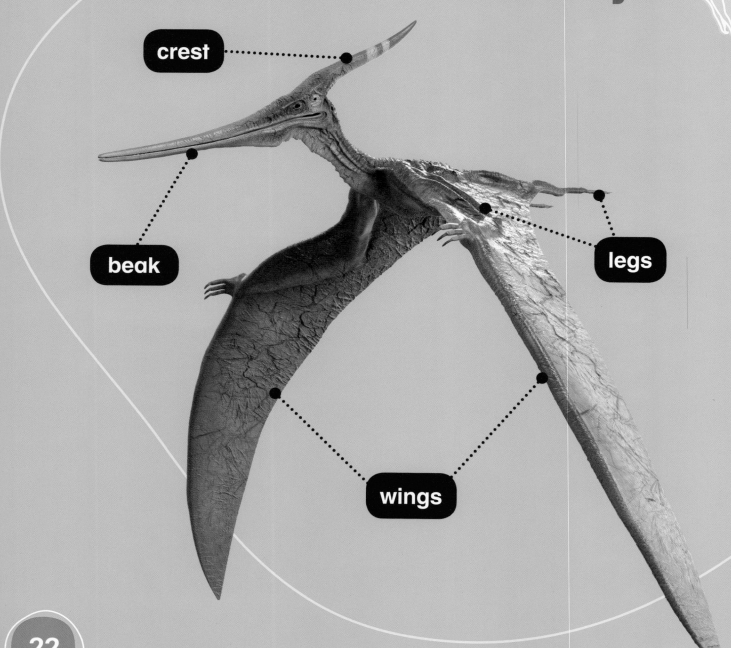

crest

beak

legs

wings

# Picture Glossary

**beak**

a hard mouth that sticks out

**crest**

a hard shape on top of the head

**extinct**

no longer alive

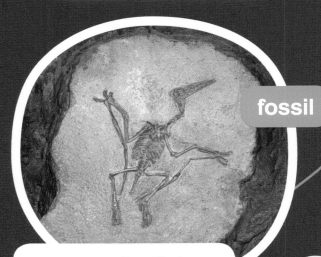

**fossil**

a trace of a living animal from a long time ago

23

# Learn More

Hansen, Grace. *Pterodactyl.* Minneapolis: Abdo Kids Jumbo, 2021.

Leed, Percy. *The Mighty Velociraptor.* Minneapolis: Lerner Publications, 2022.

York, M. J. *Dinosaurs.* Mankato, MN: Child's World, 2021.

# Index

## Photo Acknowledgments

Image credits: Sergey Krasovskiy/Getty Images, pp. 5, 23; AmeliAU/Shutterstock.com, p. 6; YuRi Photolife/Shutterstock.com, pp. 9, 23; Elena Duvernay/Stocktrek Images/Getty Images, p. 10; Elenarts/Shutterstock.com, pp. 13, 20, 23; Dariush M/Shutterstock.com, pp. 15, 23; frantic00/Shutterstock.com, p. 16; Mirt Alexander/Shutterstock.com, p. 19; Herschel Hoffmeyer/Shutterstock.com, p. 22.

Cover image: Warpaintcobra/iStock/Shutterstock.com.